My Town

by Jeri Cipriano

Scott Foresman
is an imprint of

Glenview, Illinois • Boston, Massachusetts • Chandler, Arizona •
Upper Saddle River, New Jersey

Photographs

Every effort has been made to secure permission and provide appropriate credit for photographic material. The publisher deeply regrets any omission and pledges to correct errors called to its attention in subsequent editions.

Unless otherwise acknowledged, all photographs are the property of Pearson Education, Inc.

Photo locators denoted as follows: Top (T), Center (C), Bottom (B), Left (L), Right (R), Background (Bkgd)

Opener: Ariel Skelley/CORBIS; **1** ©Bill Bachman/Alamy; **3** altrendo images/Stockbyte/Getty Images; **4** Dusan Kostic/Fotolia; **5** ©Stephen Shepherd/Alamy Images; **6** ©Ariel Skelley/Corbis; **7** ©Bill Bachman/Alamy Images; **8** Photolibrary Group, Inc.

ISBN: 13: 978-0-328-46300-8
ISBN 10:   0-328-46300-0

My town has a playground.

We climb together.

My town has a field.
We play together.

My town has a pool.
We swim together.

My town has parades.
We march together.

My town has fairs.
We eat together.

My town has neighbors.
We have fun together!